BLAZERS

TOP 10
UNEXPLAINED

TOP 10
HAUNTED
PLACES

by Lori Polydoros

Reading Consultant:
Barbara J. Fox
Reading Specialist
Professor Emerita
North Carolina State University

CAPSTONE PRESS
a capstone imprint

Blazers is published by Capstone Press,
1710 Roe Crest Drive, North Mankato, Minnesota 56003.
www.capstonepub.com

Library of Congress Cataloging-in-Publication Data
Polydoros, Lori, 1968–
Top 10 haunted places / by Lori Polydoros.
pages cm — (Blazers. Top 10 unexplained)
Includes bibliographical references and index.
Summary: "Describes various haunted places in a top-ten format"—Provided by publisher.
ISBN 978-1-4296-8435-4 (library binding)
ISBN 978-1-62065-208-4 (ebook PDF)
1. Haunted places—Miscellanea—Juvenile literature. I. Title. II. Title: Top ten haunted places.
BF1461.P65 2013
133.109—dc23   2012000115

Editorial Credits
Mandy Robbins, editor; Sarah Bennett, designer; Eric Gohl, media researcher;
    Laura Manthe, production specialist

Photo Credits
Alamy/RMUSA, 23
Corbis/Robert Holmes, 9
Dreamstime/Jruffa, 11; Russiangal, 27
Courtesy, History San José, 25
iStockphoto/Andrew Penner, 19 (back)
Library of Congress, 15, 16
Mary Evans Picture Library, 12
Newscom/Sipa Press/G. Fabiano, 17
Shutterstock/Annette Shaff, 5; Bruce Rolff, 5 (design element); Cindi L, 28–29;
    godrick, 7; Karina Bakalyan, 16 (frame); Nick Martucci, 21 (back); Olemac, 24;
    Peter D., cover; Slava Gerj, 28 (ghost); Stephen Finn, 13
Wikipedia/Steve Gustafson, 21 (front); United States Department of Justice, 19 (front)

Printed in the United States of America in Stevens Point, Wisconsin.
032012   006678WZF12

TABLE OF CONTENTS

A HAUNTING HISTORY

Have you ever noticed strange sounds, shadows, or smells? Maybe they are signs of ghosts! Spooky stories have been told throughout history. Check out the top 10 **haunted** places of all time.

haunted—having mysterious events happen often, possibly due to visits from ghosts

5

9
8
7
6
5
4
3
2
1

EDINBURGH CASTLE

In the past, prisoners were put to death at Edinburgh Castle in Scotland. In 2001 researchers took more than 200 people to the castle. Some people noticed changes in air temperature or saw strange shadows. Others felt something tugging at their clothes.

MYRTLES PLANTATION

Legend has it that long ago, a slave at Myrtles **Plantation** had her ear chopped off. Today visitors sometimes lose an earring. Staff members find the earrings where the visitors have never been! They also find chairs moved inside the locked **parlors**.

plantation–a large farm found in warm areas; before the Civil War (1861–1865), plantations in the South used slave labor

parlor–a formal living room, especially in an old house, that is used for entertaining guests

One of the Twin Parlors at Myrtles Plantation

THE QUEEN MARY

The *Queen Mary* is a floating hotel in Long Beach, California. In the past, it has been an ocean liner and a warship. Visitors say they've seen a ghostly sailor who died in the ship's engine room. Children's voices have been heard in the pool area where two girls drowned.

FACT During World War II (1939–1945), the *Queen Mary* carried more than 800,000 troops.

THE TOWER OF LONDON

Anne Boleyn was the queen of England from 1533 to 1536. Her husband, King Henry VIII, had her killed. Anne was held in the Tower of London until her death in 1536. Today soldiers there say they see and feel her spirit rush past them.

Anne Boleyn begging for her life

THE WHALEY HOUSE

The Whaley House in San Diego, California, has been a home, a store, and a theater. Many visitors have seen the ghost of **"Yankee"** Jim Robinson. He was hanged there in 1852. Others have seen the spirit of a young girl in a long dress.

Yankee–a person born or living in the northern United States, especially a state in New England

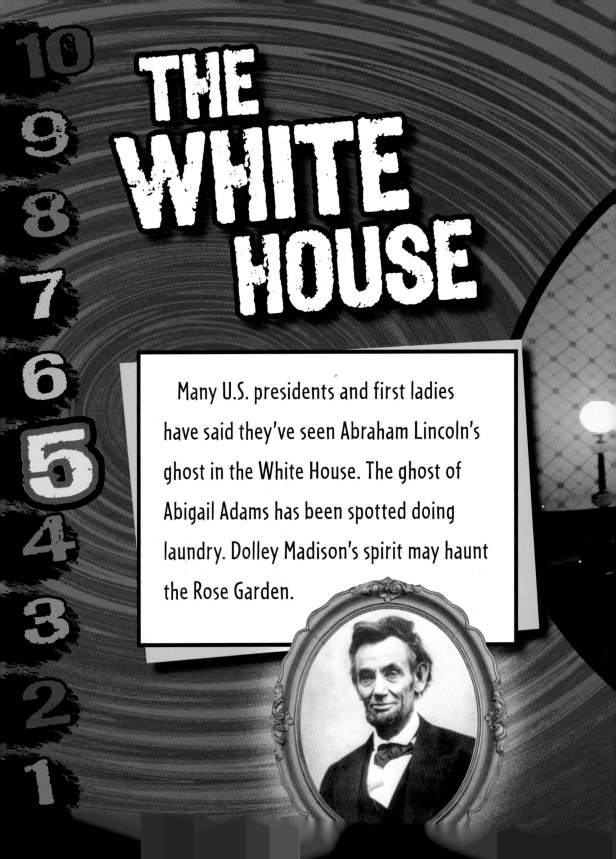

10 9 8 7 6 5 4 3 2 1

THE WHITE HOUSE

Many U.S. presidents and first ladies have said they've seen Abraham Lincoln's ghost in the White House. The ghost of Abigail Adams has been spotted doing laundry. Dolley Madison's spirit may haunt the Rose Garden.

FACT

England's former Prime Minister Winston Churchill once stayed in the Lincoln Bedroom. He said he spoke to Lincoln's ghost!

ALCATRAZ PRISON

Alcatraz was once a large prison that held violent criminals. Many prisoners died there. Guards reported moaning, strange smells, and cold spots. Ghostly forms of prisoners are still said to wander Alcatraz.

FACT The most famous ghost said to haunt Alcatraz is the gangster Al Capone.

ST. LOUIS
CEMETERY NO. 1

10
9
8
7
6
5
4
3
2
1

Marie Laveau was called the **Voodoo** Queen of New Orleans. People said she used her magical powers to help them. Marie's spirit may haunt the New Orleans cemetery where she is buried. People still visit her grave site to ask for help.

voodoo–a religion that began in Africa; voodoo combines African rituals with Christian practices

HOLLYWOOD ROOSEVELT HOTEL

The Hollywood Roosevelt Hotel may hold a haunted mirror used by Marilyn Monroe. Several people have reported seeing her face in the mirror.

10
9
8
7
6
5
4
3
2
1

FACT

Marilyn Monroe's ghost has also been spotted over her grave. She was laid to rest in Westwood Village Memorial Park in Westwood, California.

THE WINCHESTER HOUSE

Sarah Winchester's family made Winchester **rifles**. Sarah felt guilty for the deaths those guns had caused. She believed spirits had killed her family as punishment. Sarah was afraid she was next.

rifle–a gun that is fired from the shoulder and has grooves in the barrel to make bullets travel farther

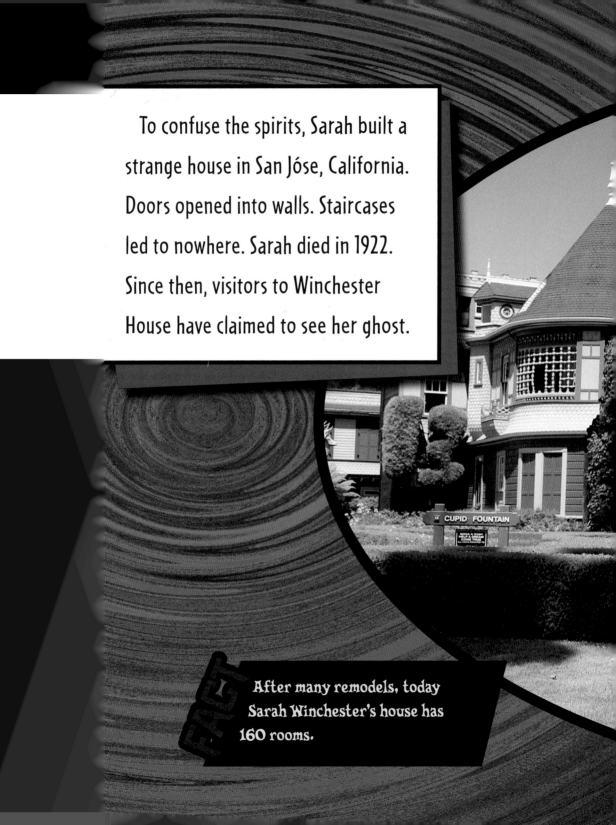

To confuse the spirits, Sarah built a strange house in San Jóse, California. Doors opened into walls. Staircases led to nowhere. Sarah died in 1922. Since then, visitors to Winchester House have claimed to see her ghost.

CUPID FOUNTAIN

FACT After many remodels, today Sarah Winchester's house has 160 rooms.

HUNTING FOR FACTS

Will we ever know if places are really haunted? Ghost hunters use special tools to look into strange happenings. Maybe one day, they will prove that ghosts are real.

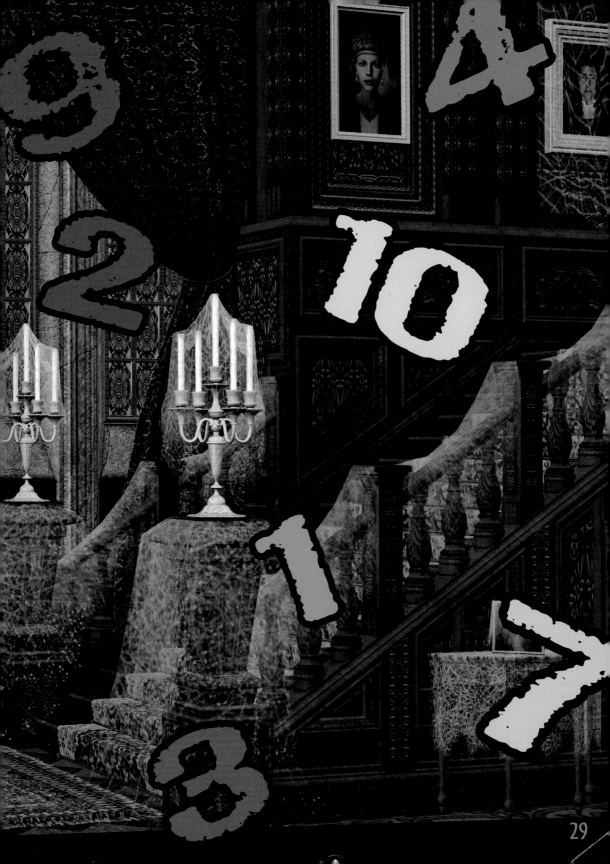

Glossary

haunted (HAWN-ted)—having mysterious events happen often, possibly due to visits from ghosts

parlor (PAR-lur)—a formal living room, especially in an old house, that is used for entertaining guests

plantation (plan-TAY-shuhn)—a large farm found in warm areas; before the Civil War (1861–1865), plantations in the South used slave labor

researcher (REE-surch-ur)—someone who studies a subject to discover new information

rifle (RYE-fuhl)—a gun that is fired from the shoulder and has grooves in the barrel to make bullets travel farther

voodoo (VOO-doo)—a religion that began in Africa; voodoo combines African rituals with Christian practices

Yankee (YANG-kee)—a person born or living in the northern United States, especially a state in New England

Read More

McCormick, Lisa Wade. *Haunted Houses: the Unsolved Mystery.* Mysteries of Science. Mankato, Minn.: Capstone Press, 2010.

Parvis, Sarah E. *Haunted Hotels.* Scary Places. New York: Bearport Pub., 2008.

Rooney, Anne. *Strange Places.* Amazing Mysteries. Mankato, Minn.: Smart Apple Media, 2010.

Internet Sites

FactHound offers a safe, fun way to find Internet sites related to this book. All of the sites on FactHound have been researched by our staff.

Here's all you do:

Visit *www.facthound.com*

Type in this code: 9781429684354

Check out projects, games and lots more at
www.capstonekids.com

Index